Just the Facts

Sickle Cell
Disease

Oliver Gillie

Heinemann Library
Chicago, Illinois

Customer Service 888-454-2279
Visit our website at www.heinemannlibrary.com

Produced by Monkey Puzzle Media
Designed by Jane Hawkins
Originated by Ambassador Litho Ltd.
Printed and bound in China by South China Printing Company

08 07 06 05 04
10 9 8 7 6 5 4 3 2 1

Library of Congress Cataloging-in-Publication Data
Gillie, Oliver.
  Sickle cell disease / Oliver Gillie.
    v. cm. -- (Just the facts)
Includes bibliographical references and index.
Contents: History -- What is sickle cell disease? -- Inheritance of sickle cell disease -- Other sickle cell disorders -- Living with sickle cell disease -- How can modern science help? -- Triumph of science and medicine.
  ISBN 1-4034-4603-2
  1. Sickle cell anemia--Juvenile literature. [1. Sickle cell anemia. 2.
Diseases.] I. Title. II. Series.
  RC641.7.S5G54 2003
  616.1'527--dc21
                                2003011027

Acknowledgments
The author and publisher are grateful to the following for permission to reproduce copyright material: pp. 1 (Alex Bartel), 5 (Eye of Science), 10 (Simon Fraser/RVI, Newcastle-upon-Tyne), 17 (Mark Clarke), 18 (Saturn Stills), 19 (Sue Ford), 21 (Ken Eward), 24 (BSIP/Laurent), 25 (St. Bartholomew's Hospital), 30 (Dr. Gopal Murti), 32 (Alex Bartel), 42 (Alex Bartel), 43 (Sue Ford), 44–45 (Alex Bartel), 47 (Dr. Rob Stepney), 49 (J. C. Revy) Science Photo Library; pp. 4, 27, 40 Topham; pp. 6, 9 Hulton Archive; p. 11 (Crispin Hughes) Photofusion; pp. 13 (Nicole Katano), 31 (Ami Vitale) Alamy; pp. 14–15, 16–17, 33 Wellcome Photo Library; pp. 22 (Taxi), 26 (Image Bank), 39 (Taxi), 51 (Taxi) Getty Images; pp. 28 (Mark Henley), 34 (Neil Cooper) Panos; p. 36 (Anthony Harvey) Press Association; artwork on p. 23 by Michael Posen.

Cover photograph: main image (blood cells): Alamy/Dennis Kunkel/Phototake Inc.; second image: Alamy/Yoav Levy/Phototake Inc

On the cover of this book, a person with sickle cell disease is shown in a hospital. Sickle cell blood cells are shown in the foreground.

Special thanks to Pamela G. Richards, M.Ed., and Marvelle Brown, Macmillan lecturer on sickle cell disease at Thames Valley University, for their help in the preparation of this book.

The case studies in this book are based on factual information. In some case studies and elsewhere in this book, names or other personal information may have been changed or omitted in order to protect the privacy of the individuals concerned.

Contents

Introducing Sickle Cell Disease

"It is unbearable. Some people who have it just want to stop living. That's how bad it is. Nothing helps the pain," says William Bratton, describing how he felt during an episode of sickle cell illness.

A fullback on the University of Toledo football team, Bratton can normally bench press 370 pounds (168 kilograms). That's about the weight of two adults! But after an episode of sickle cell illness he could barely lift 200 pounds (90 kilograms). Playing football for his college is a struggle, but he is an inspiration to his teammates.

"I get tired quicker than others. I'm gasping for air. I'm so tired I can't even drink water. It takes me two or three minutes before I have enough strength to go back out there," says William.

People who have sickle cell disease often suffer from painful attacks, which are called crises. During these crises they have pains in the arms, legs, back, and stomach that may be very severe. Their hands and feet may swell, their joints become stiff, and they feel extremely tired.

Strenuous exercise may bring on an attack of sickle cell disease.

An inherited disease

Sickle cell disease is inherited. Its name comes from the red cells in the blood of sufferers, which take on the shape of a sickle (the crescent-shaped tool used when grain is harvested by hand). People who suffer from sickle cell disease can become very ill, and that is why it is referred to as a disease. Sometimes it is called sickle cell anemia because sufferers also generally become anemic. That is, they have a reduced level of hemoglobin, the red substance in blood that contains iron and carries oxygen. Hemoglobin combines with oxygen in the lungs and then carries the oxygen throughout the body.

Sickle cells

People who suffer from sickle cell disease have a different type of hemoglobin than others. In people with the disease, hemoglobin sticks together to form long rods inside red blood cells when the oxygen supply is low. This makes the cells rigid and then they often become sickle-shaped. As these sickle cells circulate in the blood, they tend to get stuck in small blood vessels, cutting off the normal supply of oxygen and blood. This causes painful irritation and swelling, while the shortage of oxygen causes intense fatigue.

These red blood cells are from a person with sickle cell disease. The normal cells are round, while others are sickle shaped.

History of Discovery

In 1910 James B. Herrick, a doctor from Chicago, put some blood from a West Indian patient under his microscope and looked at the red cells. Among the normal round-shaped red cells he saw a "large number of thin, elongated, sickle-shaped and crescent-shaped forms," as he later told the 25th annual meeting of the Association of American Physicians.

Dr. Herrick was the first person to recognize sickle cell disease, but he was not sure what it was. The patient, Walter Clement Noel, was suffering from anemia, a disease caused by a shortage of hemoglobin, the red substance in blood. But Dr. Herrick was not sure whether the anemia from which his patient was suffering was different than other types of anemia.

Some 30 years after James Herrick discovered sickle cells, Linus Pauling (pictured here) showed that the hemoglobin of people with sickle cell disease is chemically different from the hemoglobin of other people.

The first known victim of sickle cell disease

Walter Clement Noel came from a wealthy family from Grenada in the Caribbean. He went to study at the Chicago College of Dental Surgery in October 1904. When the northern winter brought the first cold weather, he came down with a chest infection. He was admitted to the Presbyterian Hospital, where a doctor checked his blood cells and found that they were sickle shaped.

Walter Noel graduated in May 1907 and returned to Grenada, where he set up a dental practice in the capital, St. George's. Despite the sunny climate, Walter's chest problems returned, and he died in May 1916, at age 32.

Walter's case was later written up by Dr. James B. Herrick. Walter became the first known victim of sickle cell disease. If he had been a student in Chicago today, he could have expected to live twice as long.

A new disease

Five years later, two doctors at Washington University found another man with similar symptoms. They realized that they were looking at a new disease. Like the first patient, the man had African ancestors. He was also anemic and had a yellowish tinge to the whites of his eyes and ulcers on his legs. These became the classic symptoms of sickle cell disease.

In 1922, Verne Mason, a doctor at Johns Hopkins Hospital in Baltimore, Maryland, called the condition "sickle cell anemia" for the first time. The name stuck. A few years later, John Huck, who had trained at Johns Hopkins Hospital, recognized that the disease was inherited according to the laws of genetics.

It was not until 1949 that the way in which sickle cell anemia can be inherited was fully understood. James Neel, working at the University of Michigan, was then able to explain why some people had only mild symptoms. These people are carriers. They can pass the condition on to their children but do not suffer from serious symptoms themselves.

Prejudice

Many of the scientists and doctors who carried out the early research into sickle cell disease in the first half of the 20th century held racial prejudices that were common at that time.

In the early part of the 20th century, many African American people in the United States died from tuberculosis, an infectious disease that spreads easily when people live in overcrowded conditions. Tuberculosis was much more common in the African-American population than in the white population. Some people blamed a hereditary weakness of the black race. Others disagreed and pointed to the poor living conditions of many African Americans as the real cause.

Sickle cell disease was generally seen as an African-American disease. It was referred to in order to support ideas that people of African descent were less healthy than whites. These ideas were used to help justify the racist argument that white people were superior to black people.

Sickle cell in whites

Some white people in Europe and North America suffer from sickle cell disease. In the past, at a time when racial discrimination of all kinds was practiced openly, this sometimes led to their race being questioned. Or, if there was no doubt about their race, then doctors questioned the diagnosis. They found it difficult to believe that a person with European ancestors could suffer from the disease. White people who carry the sickle cell gene probably had ancestors who came from Africa. These ancestors may have been brought to southern Europe by the slave trade in ancient times. However, it is also possible that the gene originally came from more than one place.

In 1929 two American doctors reported several cases of sickle cell disease in a Greek-American family of people described as "racially pure whites." The doctors reported that the family came from "Byregos, a small village in the Peloponnisos near Olympia where their families had long been residents and where negroes are said to be unknown." If Greeks could suffer from sickle cell disease, then the disease was not limited to African-American people alone. This went against the racist argument that African Americans were naturally less healthy.

Overcrowded living conditions in countries such as the United States caused the spread of diseases such as tuberculosis among African Americans during the early 20th century.

One Disease Among Many

Individuals who suffer from chronic illness often face discrimination. People at school or work may have no idea what they are going through. Some people may believe that it is a person's own fault that he or she is ill. Others just like picking on someone they see as different.

To suffer from sickle cell disease and to be of African descent brings the possibility of double discrimination. If it is suggested that the illness is a result of racial weakness, that makes the discrimination even worse. Science no longer recognizes any such thing. All groups of people suffer from certain inherited diseases that are more common among them than in others.

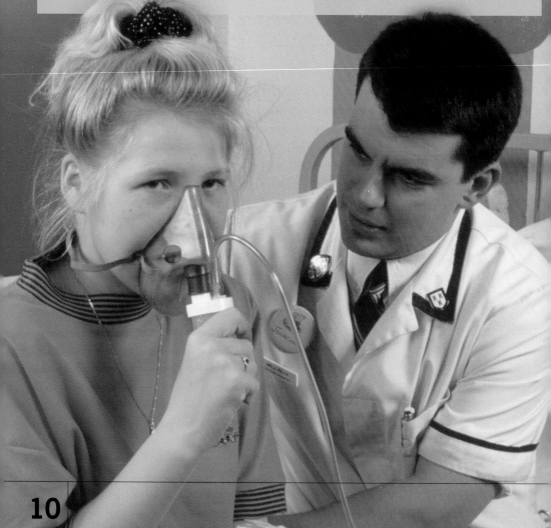

Inherited diseases

• Cystic fibrosis is an inherited disease that is much more common in people of European descent and relatively rare in people of African, Asian, or Jewish descent. About 1 in 2,500 babies with European ancestors inherit two genes for cystic fibrosis and develop the disease. They used to die in childhood from repeated lung infections. With the help of antibiotic drugs, people with cystic fibrosis today are able to live into adulthood. They are, though, often ill, and the condition often stunts their growth and reduces the length of their life.

• Tay-Sachs disease is a hundred times more common among Ashkenazi Jews (Jews of eastern European origin) than among other groups of people. About 1 in 2,500 Ashkenazi babies suffer from it. Children who are affected first show signs of the disease after about six months of age. They suffer from blindness, paralysis, seizures, and other mental disturbances. They usually die before they are four.

• Phenylketonuria is a relatively common inherited disease in people with European ancestors but rare among people with African or Ashkenazi Jewish ancestors. If the disease is not diagnosed in the first few months of life, brain damage occurs. Fortunately, it can be detected by a simple test and treated by diet. The child will then develop normally.

• Porphyria is most common among people of Scandinavian, Anglo-Saxon, and German ancestry and rare in people with African ancestors. It causes pain attacks in the abdomen and can stop the nervous system from working, leading to death. It affected Britain's King George IV (1762–1830) and other members of European royal families.

This girl with cystic fibrosis is having treatment for lung disease.

What Is Sickle Cell Disease?

Sickle cell disease affects many parts of the body. The irregular shape of the red blood cells prevents them from moving as freely through the blood vessels as normal red blood cells. They can cause blockages when they get stuck. This means sickle cells cannot carry oxygen around the body properly. Shortage of oxygen leads to damage, which is most severe in the smallest blood vessels. The damage can occur in almost any organ of the body, including the brain.

Bed rest can often provide relief from pain for people with sickle cell disease.

Pain

The disease causes extremely painful symptoms. Pain is most common in the arms, legs, back, and stomach. The joints may also become stiff and painful. Boys may suffer from a stiff, painful penis, a condition called priapism. It sometimes starts as a pain in the groin. The condition is embarrassing for them and they may not want to mention it. But it is important to seek medical help.

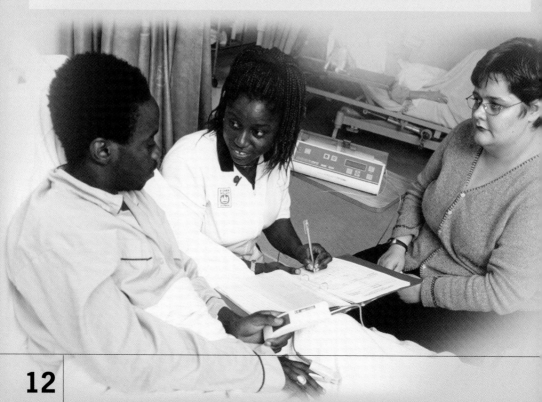

People with the disease go through good and bad periods. Most people with the disease suffer pain frequently. The pain often lasts all day and is associated about half the time with a feeling of fatigue. Children with the disease spend a lot of time in bed because rest brings some relief from exhaustion and pain.

Triggers for pain

Overexertion, overexcitement, cold weather, cold drinks, and swimming have been found by many people to trigger pains. Bumps and bruises causing damage to tissues may also trigger an attack. One parent noticed that his daughter had an attack after taking a cold drink straight from the fridge. She had less pain when drinks were served at room temperature. People with sickle cell disease should drink frequently to avoid becoming dehydrated.

Sickle cell disease is a serious condition, but it is not like other more serious diseases that sometimes cause rapid death. For example, it is not the same as cancer, in which cells in a part of the body grow out of control and form a tumor. Nor is sickle cell disease ever infectious.

Drinks served at room temperature are less likely to trigger pain among people with sickle cell disorder.

❝Finally I found out how to head off a crisis. I could feel the pain begin in my chest and back, and as it subsided in those areas the pain would travel into my arms, hips or legs, or all over my body. I now control my pain with oral Demerol tablets and oxygen, and lots and lots of fluids. ❞

(Inez Hardin, Sickle Cell Information Center, Emory University, Atlanta, Georgia)

Effects on growth

Sickle cell disease affects children's growth. Babies with sickle cell disease are born at the normal size and weight and rarely show any symptoms of the disease until after six months of age. But by the end of their first year or early in their second year, they begin to grow more slowly. They continue to grow slower than normal. As adults they may be shorter and lighter than average. Growth of bones may be as much as five years behind normal, but people with sickle cell disease do eventually catch up.

The increase in weight of children with the disease is generally slower than the increase in their height. So they tend to be slim and thin. Men with the disease tend to catch up in height by the age of 22 and women may actually be of above average height. Both men and women with the disease tend to have long, thin arms and legs, a relatively small body, and narrow hips and shoulders.

Slower development

Men and women who suffer from sickle cell disease are often slow to reach sexual maturity. Girls who have the disease may have their first period later than others—on average at age fourteen or fifteen rather than at twelve or thirteen. The age when they have their first sexual experience and their first pregnancy also tends to be later. This is probably because slower physical development means that interest in sex is delayed.

Boys with the disease are also slower to develop sexually. They have relatively low levels of the male hormone testosterone in their blood. They develop hair in their armpits, in the pubic area, and on their faces later. They may be less fertile.

Pregnancy

Women with the disease do not seem to be any less fertile than others. But pregnancy is likely to be more difficult. The risk of losing a baby is greater than normal. Women with sickle cell disease should seek medical advice early in pregnancy. Regular checkups during pregnancy will greatly reduce risks and give a better chance of a successful birth.

❝As a child I longed to be normal. Now at seventeen I understand it is something that I might never obtain . . . Life for me has been hard. I was always ashamed of who I was. I know for a fact that I am not normal compared to teens my age. I have been hospitalized over 100 times. As a child I was afraid to tell the truth about who I really am, but now I let people know because I realize that this is part of me.❞

(Heidy Dodard, Sickle Cell Information Center, Emory University, Atlanta, Georgia)

Young people with sickle cell disease, such as the boy on the left, tend to have narrow hips and shoulders.

Sickle cell crises

People who suffer from sickle cell disease have crises when the oxygen in their blood falls below 40 percent of the normal level. During these crises they suffer severe pains in their muscles, bones, and joints, as well as headaches, stiffness of the neck, and shortness of breath. They also have jaundice, a yellowing of the whites of the eyes, which is more obvious than usual. The jaundice is caused by the destruction of sickle cells, which get broken down more quickly than normal red blood cells. This leads to the production of yellow substances from hemoglobin that circulate in the blood and can be seen in the whites of the eyes.

Sickle cell crises may happen to a person with the disease at any time. These episodes of pain may be triggered by a mild infection such as a cold or flu, which cannot be predicted. A virus infection called parvovirus B19 often triggers crises. This virus circulates in the general population without causing serious illness, but people with sickle cell disease are more vulnerable to it.

Yellow eyes are a sign of jaundice. Yellow substances are formed in the body when hemoglobin from damaged cells is broken down.

Hospital treatment

When a severe crisis occurs, urgent hospital treatment is required. Generally, a person having a crisis is drowsy and cannot make decisions. Someone else may have to take the person to the hospital.

In the hospital the patient will be given pain relief. Fluids will be introduced into the body intravenously (through a vein) to correct and prevent dehydration. Antibiotic drugs will be given to prevent infection. Oxygen treatment will be given if the patient has a chest pain, which indicates that blockages are occurring in the small blood vessels of the lungs.

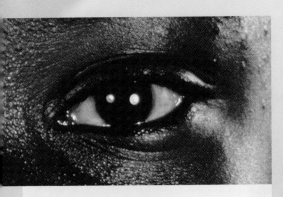

Understanding the disease

Michael Cobb grew up in Asheville, North Carolina, and as a kid he always did everything that other children did. He had many crises, but he wanted to prove that he could rise above them and so he joined the army at age eighteen.

"In my fifth week of boot camp I ran a mile and a half and went into a crisis. I felt once again my body giving way and not letting me do what I wanted to do," explained Michael.

He ended up in the depths of despair. "I was told I would not live to see the age of 35. I stopped caring about anything and everything. This led to more problems than you could ever imagine, drinking and taking drugs for about ten years."

Then he started to read about sickle cell disease. "Now at 37 I see that I could have done a lot more with my life. I never realized where I was going until I found out where I came from. It's all from the power of information."

Some or all of these signs may occur in a sickle cell crisis:

- unusually severe pains in the abdomen, spine, or chest
- headache
- stiffness of the neck
- fever
- drowsiness
- dark or red urine
- signs of possible damage to the nervous system, such as mental confusion or slurred speech

People with sickle cell disease often suffer severe pain in the abdomen.

Symptoms

The first symptoms of sickle cell disease may appear in infants at the age of six months. At about this age babies may develop fever and swollen fingers. Called dactylitis, or hand-foot syndrome, it is very painful. The swelling and pain usually disappear within a week, but appear again periodically up to age three. This may result in damage to the small bones of the hands and feet. It can lead to poor control of finger movements later in life.

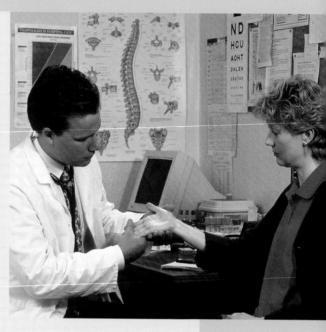

A doctor checks for anemia, which is common in people with sickle cell disease.

The spleen

Damaged red cells are removed from the blood by an organ in the abdomen called the spleen, which then recycles the hemoglobin. In children with sickle cell disease, the spleen has to work overtime and sometimes becomes choked with red cells. Very severe anemia may then follow.

From an early age, the spleen of people with sickle cell disease is unable to produce antibodies, the substances in the blood that protect against bacteria and viruses. This leaves children with the disease open to serious infections, particularly septicemia (blood-poisoning), which is caused by bacteria called pneumococci. The overworked spleen usually shrivels up and by adulthood no longer functions at all.

Bones and organs

Later in life the disease may cause damage to growing bones, especially the backbone and the hip joints. This occurs because small blood vessels in the growing ends of bones become blocked by damaged sickle cells. The damaged cells cut off the oxygen supply that is essential for living tissue.

Similar damage may occur in the kidneys, liver, bowels, and lungs, causing severe breathing difficulty and sometimes pneumonia. People with the disease often suffer from leg ulcers, caused again by the poor blood supply. And they may suffer seizures or a stroke when the brain is affected.

In Africa, few people with the disease live beyond the age of five. But in Jamaica (where good healthcare services for sickle cell disease have been pioneered) and other countries with modern healthcare services, most live into their 50s or even 60s.

❝When I was in the fifth grade I ran a mile instead of telling my instructor that I was tired. I pushed myself and as a result missed the rest of the school year. In my junior year in college I was so stressed out about a test that I ended up in the emergency room due to a sickle cell crisis.❞

(Melissa Creary, Sickle Cell Information Center, Emory University, Atlanta, Georgia)

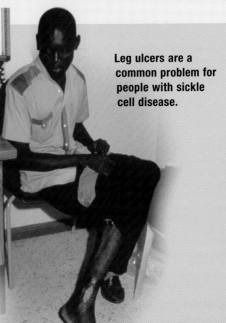

Leg ulcers are a common problem for people with sickle cell disease.

Hemoglobin

The difference between people with sickle cell disease and those without the condition is in the makeup of their hemoglobin, the red substance in blood. It has taken scientists many years to understand hemoglobin's complicated structure. They have found many different types of hemoglobin. Hemoglobin from people with sickle cell disease is called hemoglobin S.

Hemoglobin is made up of heme, which contains iron, and four globin molecules. Working together, the heme plus the four globins carry oxygen throughout the body from the lungs to other body parts, where the oxygen is absorbed. The difference between people with sickle cell disease and others lies in the globin part of the hemoglobin molecule.

The structure of globin

Globin is a protein and, like all proteins, it is made up of hundreds of amino acids joined together like links on a chain. The amino acids in any particular type of protein are arranged in a particular order along the chain, giving that protein its own special character. Globin from people with sickle cell disease differs from normal globin by just one of these amino acids in one position in the chain. The order of the amino acids in globin, and all other proteins in the body, is determined by the genes a person inherits.

In this graphic model of the hemoglobin molecule, the heme group has been highlighted in color.

Inheritance of Sickle Cell Disease

Sickle cell disease is inherited. A person suffering from the disease possesses two genes for hemoglobin S, one that has come from the father and one that has come from the mother. A child must inherit one hemoglobin gene from each parent, but otherwise it is a matter of chance which hemoglobin genes a child will inherit. Carriers inherit only one gene for hemoglobin S and one for normal hemoglobin. They generally show few signs of the disease, and their health is normal throughout life.

The genes for hemoglobin follow the laws of inheritance, as predicted by Gregor Mendel. Mendel, an Austrian monk, discovered these laws in the 1860s.

Chances that a child will inherit sickle cell genes

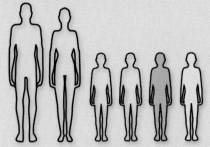

- When both parents are carriers, there is a one in four chance that a child will suffer from sickle cell disease. There is one chance in two that a child will be a carrier, and one chance in four that a child will neither have the disease nor be a carrier.

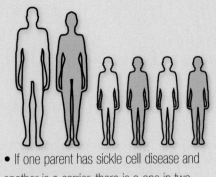

- If one parent has sickle cell disease and another is a carrier, there is a one in two chance that a child will be a carrier. The chance that a child will have the disease is also one in two.

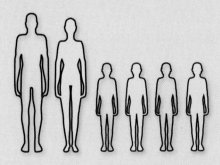

- If one parent is a carrier and the other is completely normal (neither a carrier nor suffering from the disease), there is a one in two chance that a child will be a carrier. There is a one in two chance that a child will be normal.

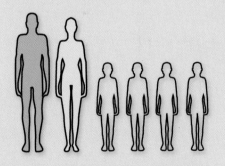

- If one parent has sickle cell disease and the other is completely normal (neither a carrier nor suffering from the disease), then all the children will be carriers.

☐ **Carrier**

☐ **Normal**

☐ **Sickle cell disease**

Tests for the Disease

The basic test for sickle cell disease can easily be done in any medical laboratory. A sample of blood is mixed with a special chemical on a glass slide and sealed with wax. The slide is left for 24 hours so that all the oxygen in the blood is removed by the chemical. If the person has the disease, the red cells then change into the sickle form and can be seen clearly under a microscope.

However, this test cannot show the difference between people who have the disease and people who are carriers. Their blood looks the same under the microscope. And the test does not work for babies because babies have only a small amount of sickle cell hemoglobin in their blood. For this reason, an electrophoresis test is generally preferred for diagnosis. In this test, an electric current is used to separate the different types of hemoglobin. It enables carriers, babies with the disease, and others with abnormal hemoglobin to be detected.

When one or both parents or any close relatives of a baby are known to be carriers, or to have the disease, a test will often be done shortly after birth. Parents can then be prepared to spot any problems that may start from about six months onward. They will also be able to take steps to prevent or minimize difficulties.

This pregnant woman is being tested to see if her baby will have sickle cell disease. The doctor uses a needle to take blood from the fetus for testing.

In electrophoresis, different types of hemoglobin are identified in the laboratory by putting a small blood sample in an electric current.

Carriers

About one in ten African Americans are carriers. In certain parts of Africa such as Nigeria, as many as one in five people are carriers. These people may be advised to have a test for sickle cell disease before they are given an anesthetic. Oxygen levels in the body sometimes become very low while under anesthetic. This can cause blood cells to sickle. It is a sensible precaution, although the risks of using anesthetic for carriers of sickle cell disease do not seem to be much greater than the risks for other people.

Tests may also be done on a blood sample from a baby or cells taken from the placenta in the early stages of pregnancy. Parents may then face a difficult choice of whether or not to continue the pregnancy.

Being a Carrier

Many hospitals test babies at birth to determine if they have sickle cell disease. But for every baby that is detected with the disease, as many as 100 carriers of the sickle cell trait may be found. These carriers have inherited only one copy of the sickle cell gene.

Carriers generally have excellent health. They live as long as other people and are no more likely than others to require hospital treatment during their life. However, in extreme conditions where there are low oxygen levels, such as on high mountains, in unpressurized aircraft, and when scuba diving, there may be an additional risk.

Carriers may experience symptoms of sickle cell disease when at high altitudes.

High altitudes

Problems have occasionally been recorded in carriers traveling in unpressurized aircraft at altitudes above 10,000 feet (3,000 meters). These vary from relatively mild symptoms of a sickle cell crisis such as backache to a blocking of blood vessels in the spleen. Similar problems could occur when climbing in high mountains, particularly if a person remained at high altitude for a long time.

Passenger aircraft are now pressurized to an equivalent altitude of 5,000 to 7,500 feet (1,500 to 2,200 meters). Problems have not been reported in carriers, although people with sickle cell disease occasionally have difficulties. Many commercial airlines nevertheless exclude carriers from jobs on the cabin crew.

Working for the armed forces

Sudden decompression can occur in military aircraft, exposing personnel to low air pressure. This risk has been considered by the armed services and employment policy toward carriers has varied. Carriers have previously been excluded from working as pilots and copilots. Today, a test of the amount of sickle cell hemoglobin in a person's blood may help to determine if an individual is suitable for the job.

A small risk of sudden death has been found in carriers during basic military training in the United States. In a study of 2 million recruits conducted by the Armed Forces Institute of Pathology, it was found that carriers were 28 times more likely to experience sudden death compared with African-American recruits who were not carriers. However, the risk of death is still tiny compared with the total number of recruits who carry the sickle cell trait. Serious problems have occasionally been reported in civilians who are carriers following intense exercise.

Military aircraft may decompress rapidly, causing problems for carriers.

Who Suffers from Sickle Cell Disease?

People with sickle cell disease and carriers of the sickle cell trait can be found all over the world. It is often believed that the disease originated in Africa, and the sickle cell gene is probably most common in West Africa. But the same disease, caused by the same gene, is frequent in India and parts of the Arabian peninsula, too. It also exists in countries around the Mediterranean, such as Greece, Turkey, and the Italian island of Sicily.

Types of sickle cell genes

In Africa, the sickle cell gene is most common among the Bantu-speaking peoples of central and southern Africa. Two main types of the sickle cell gene occur in Africa—the Benin type and the Bantu type. It is the Benin type that occurs throughout the Mediterranean. Carriers of the Benin gene probably traveled along the Sahara trade routes to Algeria, Morocco, and Tunisia. It is likely that the gene spread from there during the eighth century to Greece, Sicily, and Turkey. The high incidence of the Benin gene in Greece may be due to the fact that long ago large numbers of slaves were taken there from North Africa by the Arabs, Franks, Venetians, and Ottoman Turks.

The sickle cell gene is found all over the world and is particularly common in parts of India, such as Orissa, shown here.

The Benin gene

People with the same Benin gene were brought to North America by the slave trade between 1650 and 1830. The sickle cell trait, usually the Benin type, now occurs in eight percent of African Americans in the United States. In Brazil, seven percent of the black population carries the sickle cell trait. The gene is generally of the Bantu type because people taken as slaves to Brazil came mostly from Angola, the Congo, and Mozambique.

The sickle cell gene is very common in the large population of central India, especially in Orissa, Maharashtra, and Madhya Pradesh. It is most common among certain tribal groups: the Chetty and Kurmar of Kerala, the Abhuj Maria of Madhya Pradesh, and the Kondhs of Orissa. The gene found in India is different from the two African types.

Malaria: The Killer

Sickle cell disease is most common in the tropics, in areas where malaria is most common. Malaria is caused by a parasite that is introduced into the body by a mosquito bite. The parasite enters the red blood cells of the person who has been infected and then multiplies. The red cells burst and release the parasites, which then infect more red cells. The main symptoms are fever and weakness. The parasite sometimes invades the brain, leading to coma and death unless prompt treatment is received.

This photograph, taken with a microscope, shows a section through red blood cells (colored to show up) that have been infected with the malaria parasite.

Protective effects

People who are carriers of sickle cell disease have greater resistance to malaria than people without the gene. The benefit has been found to be greatest in young children who have not yet acquired immunity to malaria and so are most vulnerable to it.

In Accra, Ghana, children of all ages who are carriers of sickle cell disease have fewer malaria parasites in their blood than other children. In northern Ghana and Nigeria, where malaria is more severe and children gain immunity at an earlier age, the protective effect of being a carrier is limited to children under four years old. Older people and pregnant women in particular also seem to be protected by being carriers in areas where malaria is less common and immunity is not so great.

Malaria kills a million people every year in Africa. Many more die from other diseases that they develop while weakened by malaria. In these extreme circumstances, resistance to malaria provided by the sickle cell gene gives people a distinct advantage. It enables them to survive when others die.

The advantage of being a carrier

Red blood cells from carriers are more delicate than normal red blood cells. Normally they do not sickle very much and carriers generally have normal health, but the cells do tend to sickle when they are infected by the malaria parasite. These infected sickle cells are then more likely than normal cells to be filtered out by the spleen and recycled, killing the parasite.

This gives children who are carriers an extra resistance to malaria. They seem to survive better than children who are not carriers in areas that are infested with malaria mosquitoes. However, babies in rural Africa or India who inherit two copies of the sickle cell gene, and so suffer from the disease itself, generally die during infancy. Despite these deaths, the sickle cell gene remains present in large numbers of people in malarial areas because of the advantage it gives carriers.

A woman with malaria is examined by a doctor in a hospital in Uganda.

Other Sickle Cell Disorders

Hemoglobin C and beta-thalassemia

There are over 200 different types of hemoglobin disorders that have some similarity to sickle cell disease. The best known are hemoglobin C and thalassemia. These conditions do not cause pain as in sickle cell disease. Sometimes these other types of hemoglobin diseases occur together with the sickle cell gene and may then contribute to sickle cell disease.

Hemoglobin C

Hemoglobin C, or HbC, is most common in Africa, particularly northern Ghana and Burkina Faso. In the Caribbean, between two and five percent of people are carriers of the gene. People who inherit two copies of the HbC gene may have mild anemia, but they suffer few symptoms and develop normally in height and weight. However, HbC can cause serious illness in combination with sickle cell disease.

A blood transfusion is life saving for people with thalassemia.

Thalassemia

Thalassemia is common in the Mediterranean and Southeast Asia. It also occurs among African Americans. The most serious form of the disease, thalassemia major, causes hemolytic anemia—a type of anemia caused by the destruction of red blood cells. People with this disease suffer from fatigue and shortness of breath in addition to jaundice (yellowing of the whites of the eye) and enlargement of the spleen.

Thalassemia major is treated with blood transfusions, which are life-saving. But after many transfusions, the body becomes overloaded with iron, which comes from damaged red blood cells that have been recycled. This may bring on serious illnesses such as diabetes or heart failure.

This child with thalassemia is learning more about her condition.

Thalassemia major and minor

Thalassemia is an inherited disease that reduces the normal production of globin. Globin is an essential part of hemoglobin, the red substance in blood. If a person inherits one gene for the disease, he or she is deemed to have thalassemia minor, or thalassemia trait. The person is a carrier of the disease and it is not severe. If the person inherits two genes for the disease, he or she is deemed to have thalassemia major.

The evolving hemoglobin gene

For thousands of years, humans have struggled to survive in areas of Africa infected with malaria. The hemoglobin gene has evolved—gradually changed over a long period of time—to provide people with better protection against malaria. This is one of the best-known examples of human evolution.

The Dogon people

The Dogon people in Mali, West Africa, have a relatively high incidence of hemoglobin C, and it protects them from severe malaria. Dogon people who have the hemoglobin C (HbC) gene seldom suffer from cerebral malaria—a very serious form of the disease in which the parasite invades the brain. The sickle cell gene is, on the other hand, relatively rare among the Dogon people. The sickle cell gene would probably be of little advantage to them when they already have the hemoglobin C gene.

Over the centuries, African people have migrated within their continent and to other countries. As people mix and intermarry, various combinations of hemoglobin genes occur.

Dogon people, shown here enjoying a celebration, often inherit a gene that prevents malaria from attacking the brain.

Sickle cell–hemoglobin C disease

Sometimes the HbC gene occurs in the same person together with a single HbS (sickle cell) gene. That person may suffer from sickle cell disease just as if he or she had two copies of the HbS gene. These people have sickle cell–hemoglobin C disease. They suffer from the same range of illnesses as in sickle cell disease, but in a much milder form. Their growth is not usually delayed or restricted, and they generally seem to live as long as anyone else.

Thalassemia gene combinations

There are also several different thalassemia genes that can combine with the sickle cell gene. In Ghana, about one person in 800 inherits the sickle cell-beta-thalassemia combination of genes. In North America, about one in 5,000 African Americans are born with sickle cell thalassemia. In Jamaica, one in 23 babies born with sickle cell disease has the sickle cell-thalassemia combination.

In Greece, where thalassemia is much more common, roughly half of the people with sickle cell disease have the combined form. The severity of the disease varies depending on the sickle cell gene combinations inherited and other factors.

Fetal hemoglobin

In the fetus and newborn baby, a special form of hemoglobin occurs called fetal hemoglobin. It generally disappears during the first few months of life and is replaced by normal hemoglobin. However, some people have a gene that allows the fetal hemoglobin to persist in adult life. When this gene is inherited by itself, there are no problems, but when it is inherited together with the sickle cell gene a person may suffer from mild sickle cell disease.

Living with Sickle Cell Disease

T-Boz's story

"I have learned to fake a smile when I wasn't happy, to sing when I didn't feel like it, and to do things just to please my fans," says Tionne "T-Boz" Watkins, member of the band TLC.

Now a national celebrity spokesperson for the Sickle Cell Disease Association of America, T-Boz is explaining to the world how the disease has affected her life. She says: "Recently, I have learned there was a larger stage than I could ever imagine, a stage that would enable me to take my message to those who needed it most."

> **"One thing I am trying to teach kids that nobody ever taught me is that nobody's flawless. If somebody says to me that I have bags under my eyes, that I look tired, well, honey, I am tired."**
>
> **(Tionne "T-Boz" Watkins, Sickle Cell Disease Association of America)**

Childhood and teenage years

T-Boz suffered from recurring painful episodes of the illness as a child but did not know what it was until she was eight years old and the disease was diagnosed. "My attitude was . . . OK you're just going to have to face what you've got. Now suck it up and make the best of it," T-Boz told *USA Today*.

During her teen years in Atlanta, T-Boz says: "I was known as a sicko who couldn't do what normal kids were doing. I couldn't go swimming because the water was too cold, I had to drink special baby milk for my bones. I felt ugly." Concerning other teenagers with sickle cell disease she says, "There are teenagers who don't understand why they need more time to do things that normal teenagers do. There are children who may not have known until late in life about the whys of their pain."

Climbing the mountain

Her illness did not stop T-Boz from reaching the top of her profession. In 1996 TLC won two Grammy awards (prestigious awards honoring great musical achievement). In 2000 she was named by *People* magazine as one of the 50 most beautiful people in the world. But T-Boz has never felt pretty. Her painful experiences and her poor health led her to write the song "Unpretty." T-Boz says she has "climbed the mountain" herself and understands what others with sickle cell disease have to endure. She knows what it is like to go straight from a hospital to the recording studio so she wouldn't let others down.

T-Boz is now married to rapper Mack 10 and has a daughter, Chase Rolison, born in October 2000.

T-Boz (right) with fellow TLC band-member Chilli in 2002

Julia's story

Julia Aruya was born in Lagos, Nigeria. She was the only one out of four children with sickle cell disease, and her parents were told by friends to let her die. "My parents were encouraged to let me die because I was not a perfect child, a bad apple you might say," says Julia.

Her father and mother took turns taking time off work to care for her. Later, they took Julia to the United States for medical treatment. Julia graduated from college in Dallas, Texas, and got a job with a fashion retailer.

A lack of tolerance

"I worked hard so as to avoid any extra workload for coworkers in case of absence. But due to my illness and pain crises I was absent from work for 30 to 90 days in a year. If you are not at work with minimal absence you are not promotable," says Julia.

So she started a business at home, which turned out to be very successful. As a result, she was offered a new job in a multimillion dollar company with divisions all over the world. "But I found the employers lacked tolerance for someone with sickle cell disability," says Julia. "After a year of mental anguish I decided to find another position."

Like mother, like daughter

Julia returned to running her own business and also works in higher education. Her colleagues understand her problems. But now she is going through similar difficulties with her daughter, Catherina, who also has sickle cell disease.

"Her teacher actually said to me the other day: 'Catherina is such a smart child. If only she would stop lying about her stomach and her back hurting all the time. She is always in pain, always sick, always going to the nurse and this is disruptive to the class.' I went home and cried. Like me, my daughter has to fight so many battles.

"My daughter's favorite thing is ice skating. She loves horseback riding and swimming. The sky is the limit, no limitations at all. I encourage her to do and be all she can be. She wants to be a medical doctor who finds a cure for sickle cell. I pray she does." Julia wants to tell everyone with sickle cell to realize his or her potential.

Sickle cell crises can make it difficult to hold down a regular job.

The Sickle Cell Crisis

People with sickle cell disease can often tell when a crisis is coming on because their eyes begin to turn yellow (jaundice), they become thirsty, or they are more tired or irritable than usual. But there are no clear signs to show that a person is experiencing pain. Some people may suffer without saying anything about it. Children must be trusted when they say they are in pain.

The frequency and severity of crises may be reduced by practical measures. People with sickle cell disease are often advised to
• drink plenty of water and other fluids to avoid dehydration
• avoid sudden changes of temperature by always wearing plenty of warm, dry clothing
• avoid strenuous sports in cold, wet weather
• avoid swimming unless the water is warm and care is taken not to get chilled while dressing.

It is important for people with the disease to rest when they feel tired. Becoming exhausted can cause a crisis. This is difficult for children to learn because they want to keep up with their friends.

People with sickle cell disease should eat wisely and drink plenty of water.

Infections

Crises are often triggered by infections. People who have sickle cell disease should be fully immunized against common diseases such as measles. Children may be advised to take penicillin every day to avoid chest infections, which may either trigger a crisis or follow one. They are often advised to take supplements of a vitamin called folic acid, which is found in fresh vegetables and fruit. Folic acid helps the body to replace blood that is lost during the breakdown of sickle cells.

How to cope with a sickle cell crisis

A sickle cell crisis may occur quite suddenly. The person becomes sick and has severe pains in the abdomen and chest, stiffness of the neck, or drowsiness. An individual having a sickle cell crisis generally needs urgent medical attention and may be best cared for in a hospital. Powerful pain-relieving drugs can be given there.

If the crisis is not too severe, pain may be relieved at home with painkillers that can be bought over the counter in a pharmacy. Deep breathing exercises or other methods of relaxation can also help to relieve pain. Gentle massage of the painful areas may also help.

Complications

People with sickle cell disease require hospital treatment when pain cannot be controlled with medications that are available for use at home. Some painkilling drugs are restricted to use in a hospital because they are very powerful, or because they have to be given by a drip into a vein. Other complications, such as a severe chest infection, may require intensive hospital care and the injection of antibiotic drugs.

Anemia

Anemia—a shortage of hemoglobin in the blood—deprives the body of oxygen. If there is a chest infection, a common complication, this further reduces the amount of oxygen in the blood circulation. Shortage of oxygen is likely to be particularly severe in painful areas that have become swollen. In these areas, small blood vessels are blocked by sickle cells, and normal red blood cells cannot get through to supply oxygen. In the hospital, oxygen may be given to help the situation.

A person with a severe sickle cell crisis, with worsening anemia and other symptoms such as pneumonia, may need an emergency blood transfusion. This will usually be an exchange transfusion. Blood from the patient is replaced with fresh blood. This removes some of the damaged blood cells and reduces the work the body needs to do to remove them from the circulation. Patients may also receive regular blood transfusions to suppress production of sickle cell hemoglobin.

Sickle cell disease often causes ulcers on the legs and ankles, as seen here.

Priapism

Priapism—a painful erection of the penis—is another complication. This condition should be treated in a hospital. There is a danger of lasting damage if left untreated.

Bed rest

Painful bones and joints may become deformed if they continue to bear weight. So patients may be advised to rest in bed or to wear a cast to stop them from moving a limb until the inflammation goes down. Patients may be transferred home for bed rest once they are stable.

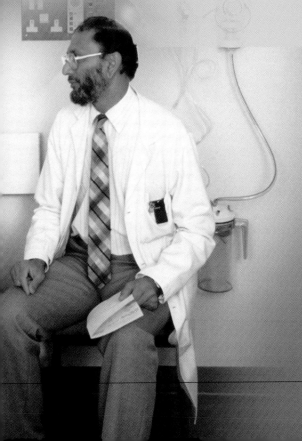

This is an eye in which the retina (the light-sensitive part) has become detached. The yellow lines are tears showing where the retina has been torn. A detached retina can be repaired.

Complications requiring hospital treatment

- pain that can't be controlled at home
- swollen, painful joints
- chest problems or pneumonia
- interruption of blood supply to the bowels
- severe swelling of the spleen or liver
- inflammation of the gallbladder
- kidney pain or blood in urine
- unwanted erection of the penis
- blood inside the eye
- detachment of the retina
- severe headache or convulsions
- signs of a stroke, such as dizziness, confusion, or slurred speech

New Treatments

New drugs bring hope

Progress in clinical science and techniques in the last ten years have brought greatly improved treatment for patients with sickle cell disease. Infections, brain injury, kidney disease, pain, and priapism can all be prevented most of the time.

Hydroxyurea

One of the most effective ways of reducing the sickling of cells is to increase the amount of fetal hemoglobin in the circulation. Fetal hemoglobin is produced in the fetus and in babies. Normally, very little is produced after the age of six months or a year, but production of fetal hemoglobin can be stimulated with drugs.

Hydroxyurea is a drug prescribed in the United States for people who have frequent crises and show the first signs of damage to organs. It increases the production of fetal hemoglobin by acting on the cells that make hemoglobin. Hydroxyurea has been found to reduce pain episodes, lung problems, and admissions to the hospital in about 60 percent of patients with these problems.

Nitric oxide

A number of other drugs are being produced for patients who do not respond to hydroxyurea. A particularly promising new approach is being developed in experiments with mice. A gas, nitric oxide, has been found to prevent the dehydration of cells and the formation of sickle hemoglobin into rods. Nitric oxide also makes it more difficult for sickle cells to pile up and block small vessels. Nitric oxide can be given as a drug, arginine, which forms the gas in the body.

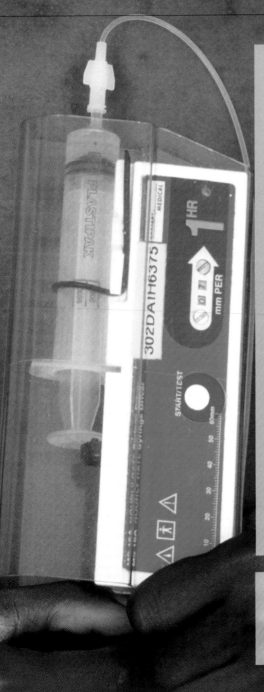

Blood transfusions

Better ways are also being discovered to give blood transfusions, which are necessary when anemia becomes very severe. A process called apheresis avoids overloading the patient's body with iron. This removes damaged red cells from the circulation. When frequent blood transfusions are given, patients often begin to react to donated blood. Suitable donors become more difficult to find. Now that this is understood, blood can be matched more carefully and these difficulties can be avoided.

Together, these new approaches to treatment and new drugs provide substantial overall improvements for some patients. However, people with sickle cell disease still spend much of their lives in the hospital, and on and off drugs such as painkillers and antibiotics.

This drug pump used in the treatment of sickle cell anemia shows the catheter visible under the skin. It pumps a drug into a vein above the heart, which makes body iron dissolve so it can be passed from the body.

Bone marrow transplantation

Transplanting bone marrow, the body tissue that produces red blood cells, offers the possibility of a cure for sickle cell disease. If normal bone marrow can be grown in someone with sickle cell disease, it will produce normal red blood cells that will replace the sickle cells. But this procedure can be done only when a suitable donor is available.

The treatment involves considerable risk because the bone marrow of the person with the disease must first be destroyed by radiation. Until the bone marrow transplant has multiplied and reached sufficient size, a process that may take a few weeks, the patient lacks resistance to infection. He or she can easily die from a minor viral infection.

Because of the risk, bone marrow transplants are generally considered only for people who suffer more extreme forms of the disease. These include those who have suffered a stroke, because there is a high risk of it happening again with severe or fatal results. Serious chest symptoms, which have a high risk of fatal complications, are another reason. People with frequent painful crises are considered, too. The procedure is generally only offered to patients under 24 years old in the United States and under 16 years old in the United Kingdom. Younger patients are healthier and more likely to survive the procedure.

Finding a donor

In order to transplant bone marrow, a suitable donor with matching body tissues, usually a relative, must first be found. Donors who are not related to the patient are now also being used in some hospitals, enabling more people to benefit. But donors must have body tissues that closely match those of the patient. Experience in the United States has shown that a donor can be found for only about one in five patients.

The success rate

The transplant procedure is successful in over 80 percent of patients. Painful crises no longer occur, their lungs work better, and damage to their bones stops. A normal life becomes possible for them.

However, about seven percent of patients who undergo the procedure die. Sometimes the grafted cells die and the patient is left without any working bone marrow. Sometimes the transplanted cells turn against the patient and attack body tissues with fatal results. And sometimes the radiation causes other complications.

Another ten percent of patients for whom the transplant is not successful survive the procedure. However, their treatment may not be a complete failure. Some patients have found that the condition is milder even though their transplant is not working properly.

Steady improvement in results can be expected in years to come as understanding of the difficulties increases. At present, bone marrow transplantation represents the best hope of a complete cure.

During a bone marrow transplant, bone marrow from a carefully matched donor is injected into the patient.

Gene therapy

If the gene for normal hemoglobin could be inserted into the cells of people with sickle cell disease, the condition might be cured. That is the goal of gene therapy. Work began on gene therapy in 1979, and some twenty years later scientists began to get positive results. The first experimental treatments in human beings may begin in 2005.

Human genes into mice

Philippe Leboulch is a scientist working at the Massachusetts Institute of Technology and Harvard University. After working on the problem for ten years, Leboulch succeeded in transferring human genes into mice that had been transplanted with human cells producing sickle cell hemoglobin. The technique involves transferring genes by attaching them to a virus. The virus is then used to infect the bone marrow of the mice. The bone marrow is targeted because that is where the body makes red blood cells.

Successful gene therapy

The first successful results were obtained by Michel Sadelain at the Memorial Sloan-Kettering Cancer Center in New York. Sadelain used gene therapy to correct thalassemia in mice. A year after the correction was made, the mice were still producing normal hemoglobin. In 2001 Leboulch was able to correct sickle cell disease in mice using an antisickling gene. The mice remained healthy, with improved production of hemoglobin a year later.

A long way to go

However, big problems must be resolved before the therapy can be made suitable for people. The virus used to carry the gene into the mice was a form of HIV, the virus that causes AIDS. There is a question whether this might have bad effects on people in the long term. Better ways are also needed of removing unhealthy cells from bone marrow before fresh cells carrying the new gene can be inserted. Many more safety tests are needed before treatment of people can begin.

Human genes have been transferred to this mouse, carried into its body by a virus.

" Everybody thought that sickle cell disease would be the first to be cured by gene therapy, that it would be simple. But it has turned out to be completely different. It was a real challenge.**"**

(Philippe Leboulch, Massachusetts Institute of Technology)

Hopes for a Cure

Today, with modern drugs and better understanding of the disease, many people with sickle cell disease can live into their 50s and 60s. The pain that generally accompanies the disease is still difficult to control. But a deeper understanding of the disease has provided better guidelines for management.

Research

Research into sickle cell disease has been intensive. It has provided the best-known example of human evolution in action—the struggle of the human body to fight the malaria parasite. But research in the lab has been slower to produce benefits for people who have the disease.

Some people have argued that progress in producing new treatments for sickle cell disease would have been faster if as many white people suffered from the condition. This may well be true. Yet progress has also been slow in finding remedies for other inherited diseases.

Only in very recent years have hopes of a cure been raised. Bone marrow transplants may now bring a complete cure for a few people. Gene therapy could also provide a cure for some people. If this is achieved in the next decade, it will be a great triumph of science and medicine. Yet there are still important practical problems to be solved. The shortage of suitable donors and the high cost is likely to restrict such treatments to a minority of people in Europe and North America.

More understanding

In rural Africa and India, it will almost certainly continue to be a miracle if babies with sickle cell disease survive beyond childhood. For most people with the disease, including those in Europe and North America, substantial benefits may come from better application of the knowledge we already have. Increased understanding of new drugs and when they are best used, and early recognition of the disease, will also bring benefits for many people.

Today, young people who have sickle cell disease will commonly live into their 60s. The future will hopefully bring new and even better treatments that improve the quality of life for people with the disease.

Patient groups, which are increasingly influential, campaign to make sure that the best management methods are applied to patients in all social groups. They educate doctors and the public to help them understand how to help people with sickle cell disease today, not just in the future.

Four children with sickle cell disease

"Both of my parents are carriers," says Santina Green, who was raised in Columbus, Ohio, "and I am the oldest of four children, three girls and a boy, who all have sickle cell disease.

"My parents had the hardest times looking after four children with the disease and trying to work as well. We were all patients at the Columbus Children's Hospital, where we have all been with pneumonia and had several blood transfusions. I would like to applaud both my parents for making sure we all got through school without being held back or having bad grades.

"Now my sisters and I all have children and they are all carriers. I thank God for that everyday."

Information and Advice

Patient groups are important sources of help for people of all ages with sickle cell disease, their relatives, and friends. At these groups, patients can share information, discuss problems, and find new solutions. They pool their resources, get experts to come and talk, and most importantly, provide understanding for each other. They also provide information, which ranges from details about other people's experiences and advice on day-to-day care through to high-level technical information.

Contacts

Sickle Cell Information Center
P.O. Box 109
Grady Memorial Hospital
80 Jessie Hill Jr. Drive SE
Atlanta, Georgia 30303
Phone: 404-616-3572
Website: www.scinfo.org/
The Sickle Cell Information Center can provide information and a list of contacts, including educational materials.

Sickle Cell Disease Association of America
200 Corporate Pointe, Suite 495
Culver City, California 90230-8727
Phone: 310-216-6363
Website: www.sicklecelldisease.org/
The Sickle Cell Disease Association of America provides sickle cell research, education, and social services. On the organization's website you can meet the association's spokesperson, Tionne "T-Boz" Watkins.

Websites

Have a Heart for Sickle Cell Anemia Foundation
http://4sicklecellanemia.org
This not-for-profit organization's goal is to improve the quality of life of those affected by sickle cell disease.

Fight Sickle Cell Disease
www.fightscd.com
This website is dedicated to fighting sickle cell disease.

Dolan DNA Learning Center
www.yourgenesyourhealth.org
This multimedia guide to genetic diseases includes information on sickle cell disease and beta-thalassemia.

More Books to Read

Gold, Susan Dudley. *Sickle Cell Disease.* Berkeley Heights, N.J.: Enslow Publishers, 2001.

Harris, Jacqueline L. *Sickle Cell Disease.* Brookfield, Conn.: Millbrook Press, 2001.

Ross, Allison J. *Everything You Need to Know about Anemia.* New York: Rosen Publishing, 2000.

Sacerdote, Alan. *Hope and Destiny: A Patient's and Parent's Guide to Sickle Cell Anemia.* Belvidere, Ill.: Hilton Publishing, 2001.

Glossary

amino acid
substance that combines in long chains to form proteins

anemia
medical condition in which someone has too little hemoglobin in the blood cells

anesthetic
substance that lessens or removes feelings and sensations, including touch and pain

antibiotic
drug that kills bacteria or prevents their growth and that can cure infections

apheresis
process that separates cells in the blood and returns the good cells to the body

bacteria
microbes that can cause infection

carrier
person who can transmit a disease but does not have the disease

circulatory system
system in which blood circulates throughout the body. The heart, arteries, and veins together are known as the circulatory system.

crisis
attack of sickle cell disease

dactylitis
inflammation and swelling of the fingers

dehydration
loss of water from the body

discrimination
unfair treatment based, for example, on a person's color, religion, ethnic group, gender, or medical health

fertile
in men: able to impregnate a woman; in women: able to get pregnant

fetus
baby in the early stages of pregnancy

folic acid
vitamin found in fresh green vegetables that is essential for normal growth and multiplication of cells

gene
part of chromosomes that carries instructions for how the body develops and carries out life processes

genetics
scientific study of the ways in which different features are passed down from parents to children

globin
molecule in blood. Four globin molecules join together with a heme molecule to make a hemoglobin molecule.

heme
molecule that joins together with four globin molecules to make hemoglobin

hemoglobin
red substance in blood, made up of one heme molecule and four globin molecules

hormone
substance produced in the body that influences how the cells and tissues function

immunity
body's ability to avoid infection and fight off disease

inflammation
condition in which a part of the body becomes red, sore, and swollen because of infection or injury

jaundice
condition in which the whites of the eyes and the skin become yellow because the body cannot dispose of a yellow-brown substance, bilirubin, which accumulates in the blood

malaria
serious and sometimes fatal disease caused by a parasite in the blood

molecule
smallest unit of a chemical

parasite
creature that lives in or on another creature

pneumonia
inflammation of the lungs caused by infection

prejudice
negative feelings toward a group of people that are not based on factual information

priapism
painful erection of the penis

protein
large molecules made up of hundreds or thousands of amino acids linked in chains. It is needed for growth and to repair damaged parts of the body.

seizure
brief spell in which the messages inside the brain get mixed up and the person loses control of his or her body

septicemia
poisoning of the blood caused by infection

spleen
organ that removes worn-out blood cells from the circulatory system and that fights infection

stroke
damage to part of the brain caused by a lack of adequate blood supply

testosterone
male sex hormone that is produced by the testes

thalassemia
inherited blood disease in which hemoglobin is not produced in the normal quantity

tissue
mass of cells that form the different parts of humans, animals, and plants

trait
condition that is inherited

transfusion
transfer of blood into a person's body to replace blood lost in an accident or to correct anemia

ulcer
open sore on the skin

virus
tiny microbe that causes infectious disease

Index